THE COTTAGE
BUILDER'S LETTER

BOOKS BY GEORGE MURRAY

Carousel: A Book of Second Thoughts (2000)
The Cottage Builder's Letter (2001)

THE COTTAGE
BUILDER'S LETTER

GEORGE MURRAY

M&S

CANADIAN CATALOGUING IN PUBLICATION DATA

Murray, George, 1971-
The cottage builder's letter

Poems.
ISBN 0-7710-6672-4

I. Title.

PS8576.U6814C67 2001   C811'.6   COO-932933-1
PR9199.3.M87C67 2001

We acknowledge the financial support of the Government of Canada through
the Book Publishing Industry Development Program for our publishing
activities. We further acknowledge the support of the Canada Council for the
Arts and the Ontario Arts Council for our publishing program.

ONTARIO ARTS COUNCIL
CONSEIL DES ARTS DE L'ONTARIO

Typeset in Aldus by M&S, Toronto
Printed and bound in Canada

McClelland & Stewart Ltd.
The Canadian Publishers
481 University Avenue
Toronto, Ontario
M5G 2E9
www.mcclelland.com

1 2 3 4 5   05 04 03 02 01

For my father

Contents

III

IV

I

A Good Life in the Converted Church

When the not-yet-father asks no one in particular, *Who sells
a church?* the not-yet-mother slaps him absently
on the arm, rubs her belly, turns back to the unkempt grounds
filled with wild ivy, hoary willows, poplars, aged swords
of grass, impressions in the earth that might be graves;

and there, between the cedar post fences of the converted
schoolhouse and the converted mill they pause, think
of how this could be the last remaining mark of other lives
that once stood at the concession corners, and how
everything at one time was about the coming to crossroads;

and in anticipation they see how the yard will soon be full
of lumber, a real family being built from a woman who bleeds,
a child who laughs and cries, a father who works
at everything with his callused hands: a loft for sleeping,
shutters covering the stained glass, the arch of his wife's back.

There will be sinning: swearing, drinking, sex for the hell of it,
gluttony, laughter at the misfortune of others, parents cursed,
people used; there will be heated words spoken in bed,
brazen dancing, teachings of an evolution outside the Garden,
envy, scraped knees healed with plain kisses and time;

there will be adultery, a theft of silverware, a murderous
incident between parakeet and cat, sloth, sore knuckles,
picked flowers, a first kiss, a black eye, hatred, a last kiss,
sickness that spreads under the skin, an obituary that reads
like plans for another home, one never built.

And yet, even as the inside is gutted in their mind:
the not-yet-father tearing down pews, laying kitchen counters
over the pulpit where chickens and lambs will be spread,
pasting untaken photos into a curling black album, ripping
up the old floor and replacing it with new hardwood slats;

the not-yet-mother raking fifty years of unfallen leaves
from the garden of thyme, wort, peonies, and harebell,
building a bedroom in the choir loft where the top ten feet
of stained glass may shed a light patterned of saints
and sinners on the four-posted bed they can't yet afford;

the question gets answered by the steeple: the Christ-figure
hanging above the bell tower using the cross as a crutch
to keep himself from falling to earth, his final moments spent
watching as he always wished he could and working
as a simple weather vane that only warns of one kind of storm.

The Last of the Sinners Waits on a Rock for Noah

I stood with the calm of a hunting stork,
the patience of a scarecrow: arms outstretched
for balance, one foot drowned to the ankle
in the floodwaters, the other tucked
inside a knee, one sole gripping my leg,
the other palming like a fist that highest peak.

I lost count at forty days, but still know this –
by twenty the water had chased us up here,
by thirty the heads of my people had sunk below
the rain, by forty memory deserted me
to the awareness I was now all body: bones
and skin waterlogged and dried into this pose.

Around me at times birds flew: sparrow,
split-tailed swallow, nightingale and thrush,
each winging on its last breath
then spinning down into the sea –
never one with a moment's thought given to
saving itself on an arm where blood still flowed.

Sometime recently, I couldn't say when,
a strong but, later I learned, unfaithful crow
came gliding just above the hushed surface –
its cry petulant, as though tired of carrying
the sky: those ailerons, suited to soaring,
camouflaging it like a thief against the Black Sea.

And in its flight, so curiously near, I caught
sight of a dark eye as it closed the distance
to pluck and eat from my hair a twig and leaf,

another determined refugee of the water,
perhaps an only remaining relative,
and in that gleaming oculus I was revealed –

salt flats like a teary desert of dry riverbeds
stretching back from my eyes, cracked
white tide rills running like fossilized evidence
of earthly trauma across my desiccated lips,
a bleached crown of black hair withered
and hardened, standing from my head.

And, as I started in fright at the face
of a stranger, the fickle crow flew off unfed,
its wings disappearing over the horizon,
and I was alone again, for a time, until
a seemingly tame rock dove swept in, lighting
on the taut and burnt muscles of an arm –

its slim, peaked body heaving with just
enough breath to keep alive the twitching
of its head, and it stayed a moment
preening and warbling, rummaging for food
among the jetsam of my beard: only
relief, good intentions, and hunger in its eyes.

But in its fearless fetching of leaf and branch,
the balance I had for so many days struck
between me, the mountain, and the sea
was broken: and slowly, with a creak in
the bones like a keel in a storm,
                                        I began to tip.

In the apology of its stare, also reflecting
both myself and the blue-on-blue horizon,

another scene played before it too fled –
widening eyes, a scorched head tilting away,
the skyline listing to an angle viewed
most often by the awakening and the dead.

MEMORIES OF THE SNAKE

My father has always been afraid of snakes,
of their long muscular bodies lying close
to the earth, of how they can taste the planet

from low currents of air across thin tongues –
he despises how their lidless eyes see
things his do not, their chiselled heads

working as basins for mysteries dirt has known
since well before him –
it's a fear he has been mute with

through almost every year I've known him –
yet once when I was a child, I remember
walking with him through a thicket garden

where I found a tiny serpent overturned
in the deepest bush, its pale underbelly exposed
to the sun, its dry, dead tongue lolled

across the path beneath us, sense memories
soaked back into the soil –
This is how secrets are kept so long, I thought

and, hooking it over a long stick,
its body draped limp over the thin fulcrum
of twig, I held it up to him at arm's length,

unaware of the reaction to come –
his recoiling head, skinless eyes, bared teeth,
his body twisting away as though tearing itself

off at the top –
Get it the hell away! he yelled,
throw it back where it came from! (what I recall

first when I remember that day is the scent
of the thicket, a lilac bush nearby)
But it's dead, I replied, it can't hurt you –

It could once, he spit, sniffing out my lie,
and that's enough for me.

THE COTTAGE BUILDER'S LETTER
(Muskoka, 1903)

i: There are things behind as well

like the nothing he can't think of telling just yet;
he hasn't written a letter in so long
and there's no telling where it might go –

like the blocked runnel road; the late-afternoon sun
behind a line of boxcars stalled north to south
on the track, a row of homes with open doors –

like autumn; it was summer when he left,
and he touches a last dazed yellowjacket drunk
on the chill, its sting fallen into his ink pot –

like the peach-blush twilight south and west,
a skin of light over the collapsed barns and homes
on rural routes; the moon tipping in –

like a night where trees and people at the roadside
become dark, armless windmills,
the gears inside turning soundlessly –

like solid rock pushing up between the trees,
moss, and scree; space for a cabin or shooting stars,
every streak of light passing behind him –

like the man who plucked him, fresh off the boat
at lakeside, hungry but still able
to swing a hammer; a fist full of broken knuckles –

(There has never been a moon so thin;
such an abundance of everything to build on
                                    but this)

like a knock on the door whose frame isn't built,
a hand on the knob that is only a thought,
a folding knife or a pen opened in a shallow pocket.

ii: Before the work begins there is too much to think of

like the two other men also arrived who have written
long letters home to sisters, children, wives –

like the mistake of leaving the steady gruel of the boat
to pretend anywhere his shadow cast was home –

like shouts from the drunk architect planting stakes
in the soil, painting glyphs on trees and rock –

like the wait for workers to arrive that stretches
into weeks; the food dwindling to apples and berries –

like a thought of sisters left searching for husbands
on the streets of Belfast; any man with pennies enough –

like the hope that sometime before the wood arrives
there will come to him words that will not defy pen –

like seven midnights with stars blocked by clouds;
a growing hunger and worry like childhood –

like a change of month; another week that passes
without a word sent home or sight of a single nail –

like age ten, stealing from the collection plate at church:
ha'penny in from the fingers, penny out in the knuckles –

(the islands dry out, the bay-waters lower; the architect,
                    cursing the dry summer,

knows the boats can't pass, sets them to hunting;
      but no one is yet so hungry as they were)

like fearing that when finally able to lie down, the letters,
like food and men, might go, or come from, nowhere.

iii: What is brought to him he remakes with his eyes

like the local steamer hauling wood from the mills downriver
through the blocked shoals, black smoke as though from a pipe cast
overhead, and rafted in from there; the wet wood a silent passenger,
its knotted mind on those it knew and what it would say if it could –

like the crates of black spikes, the boxes of spruce-handled saws
and hammers wrapped in oilcloth, the hand-mixed mortar;
the corn-dough a hired black cook bakes into travel bread, the raw
onions to feed the Russian mason and the woolly carpenter –

like the letters the Jewish boy brings to him for spelling, every other
word sounded out between them; apple; the thick dark script
of the charcoal blurred by his three-fingered left hand passing over
what is written, paper smoky as lantern glass where unfinished –

like the American woodcutter that arrives by raft from the mill,
chopping for food: a recession making axemen too costly to pay;
the cedar frame for a windowsill brought in scattered pieces yet
still standing out like a face hidden amid the planks and timber –

(would that he were a painter or some other skilled in light and were
able to tell each item for what it was;

yesterday, ten words pooled
in his head but hunger and the night drove them off unpenned)

like the fat fox-snake speared with a nail on a long stick, thrashing
in the wet fecund air, its own sharp stink, and the sour smell of men;
held over the fire and made ash, the dark tunnel of its skin
fallen in to become the lead of a pencil held at the ready arm's end.

iv: Up the hill they move from the wood-raft

like thoughts pressed down into his mind by the planks;
each step a struggle in the wind-scarred rock –

like the merciless red ants that run in the tide rills
of the rock; their throbbing little lives –

like the running water far behind the site lined up
at a beaver dam to pass into the interior lake; but held –

like the muskrat who lies on its back cracking open
mussel shells; inside each only a pearl of flesh –

like the heavy clouds that after the first day
block the sky; the lake only able to mirror stillness –

like the mouth of rocks on the long island seething
with slim garter snakes; one thick rattler waiting outside –

like the month that passes by, from new moon to new
moon, without a shred of blue sky; yet dry as sand –

like the water lilies, flowerless, their stems stretching
inches out of the low water to suspended pads; roofs –

like the smoke of mosquitoes and blackflies that blinds him
from the plan; dry air and time beginning to kill them off –

(he can feel it as he hauls up the last of the supplies;
                                        the waiting)

like the first rain in weeks hitting the pale grey stone;
each drop spreading the deepest Indian indigo –

like the night before the work begins; the silence of sky
torn open for a moment to the last, or first scrap of moon.

v: Rain ready in the clouds

like a child-laden belly, the mother stooped
in a birthing squat right there amid the blighted
potatoes; seven-year-old girls helping her sit,
an absent husband drunk to six months from dead –

like the men now assembled, waiting for light,
for any signal to begin building;
the evening fire a ring of laughter that works
as well as any walls against the black woods –

like the answers to questions after weeks
of wondering: how trees can grow on the oldest
stones, where men made homes here
without the tradition of ruin –

like yesterday's encounter with the black bear,
its deep huff in the woods a few feet off
as he made water near a shelf of rock; the wet
sound of its feeding, the sharp scent of its departure –

like the thought that tomorrow at least something
will happen; that, even as the stars turn behind
the dark clouds, so much time having been lost,
they are at the nail; the sound of birds –

(he put his hand on a tree, almost thought he felt
a pulse; the air thick as though
                        from a slow leak of steam)

like the blue moss and lichen rolled in long strips
from the rock, the digging bear having taken the grubs,
but left a new world of earth exposed to the sun;
wind, drops of rain, and the seeds from above.

vi: Between the hammer and the nail there is air

like the memory of an arched door near Tara, a bolt-hole
through which he ran as a child; famine a knotted fist,
a heavy riveting glove, a lump of molten metal in his stomach –

like the memory of fleeing his apprenticeship, the black forges
steaming in massive teakettle bursts; his mother's drawn face
counting pennies, his father's tiny marker grown over with grass –

like the memory of leaves dying near the furnaces
of Liverpool; a crisp brown halo, an aura around
the green, so unlike the ruddy apple turning seen here –

like the memory of the long boat, the heat of the boiler room,
the hammock thickly polluted by hundreds of other bodies;
looking into daylight after weeks under a dark metal sky –

like a memory of first days in this country, sleeping
in fields, under porch stoops, in missions and caves;
the stony sound of water or the watery sound of stone –

like the memory of switching from steel to wood, pipefitting,
drilling, the heat of steam through metal left behind; bending
his mind on anything, even wood, better than starving in Ireland –

(there is finally a moment of no thought before his hand begins
to descend, the torque creating a vacuum –
                    everything he ever wanted pulled in)

like a clear memory of his own unscarred, childhood hands
held out before him, the skin unbroken and unlined, the knuckles
bending without pain or resistance; good tools kept poorly.

vii: Everything about is not the cottage

like the thoughts he has been chewing for weeks, mulling in
the corners of his teeth as tobacco leaves, worrying
with his tongue; speaking not an option and it is too wet to write –

like the bear, the potential for spring in its hunting crouch,
muscle on muscle sliding under a hidden skin as it stares
into the rain-pocked lake; what reflection there is distorted –

like the hand-cut planks laid in staggered piles
next to live towers of pine; a saw, not forgotten but rusting
near one end, stuck on angle like an axe –

like the soft mounds of wood-dust coloured light as owl-down,
sand, or the inside mount of an acorn cap tipped and rolled up
as though fallen off in rest; a worker's bed now mud wet –

like the crested ducks bobbing quietly offshore, the colour
of leather, the colour of sun on the rocks, the colour of dark
shapeless openings in the hillside; mouths with clusters of teeth –

like the rain, almost alive, coming in hard sheets of warm water
as though to clean the dead; the stone made treacherous,
porous, streaming like sweat on brows and cheeks –

like the lull when the clouds seem to be higher, a tower
now just bored to death of rain –

                              (the words have lost their taste
and the spit is vile and black; there will be weather for letters
tomorrow)

like how in the silence, before the air can recover, the first axes
hit the stone ringing, or the first axes hit the ringing stone.

II

THE BRIDGE

From the back of an old book falls a photograph
he forgot to label – one without context, taken
months ago when he was sick with a traveller's fever –

a man at the base of a Roman bridge, some Italian town's
clock tower peeking from the background. Whether it's
him is impossible to know, and he can't remember,

the distance is too great – the body hidden like a tiny
fly in the dry river's gloom. Yet squinting,
he can almost make the figure out – its back leaned into

the cornerstone, arms above the head in a sloppy V,
the grey brickwork towering up. He can't quite
be sure, but the shadowed man could be

a smiling tourist using his body for scale –
or a muscular worker left to hold the tons of stone
upright while others run for cover – or maybe

it's the ghost of a sentry still guarding the grounds
from thieves.
                    But perhaps most frightening is to think

that it may be a jumper caught just before impact –
a daredevil who leapt into the murk not knowing
the river had dried – body cutting tautly

through the air, delusions of grandeur swimming
with sickness in circles below the skin, ready to bust open
into clouds of sweet confetti or candy-white wings.

If it is him, he wonders, where would the questions
have gone, swept away under that waterless bridge?

Two Hundred Acres: First Draft of a Coroner's Report

In this town it can take almost eight hours to find a man
in two hundred acres of trails and bare trees,
even with clear footprints broken through the snow –

locals and relatives pulled out of bed, searching side by side
with a bleary-eyed constable, a visiting Red Cross worker,
a ploughman who couldn't get fuel on Christmas morning.

Understand that there is the thinly iced creek to think about,
winding through the bush, invisible under the drifts
except by the evenness of snow and the lack of trees,

so much like the one our victim fell through to the left hip,
the outing at that point still just a walk in the woods
with the dog, every other track after that a limp –

and there's the trespassing hunters he tried to scare off,
beer swilling and willing by dark to shoot at anything,
it was they who shamefully led investigators to where

his loaded .22 was found leaned against a tree,
fingerprints torn off on the black metal of the barrel,
the dog's tracks doubling back home from there –

and then there's those packs of small brush wolves yipping
in the distance, attracted to the scent of failure,
of sweat, of cold kidneys, of swatches of frozen piss

come out as yellow slush and ice pellets spread over

the snow, red flakes of a urethra's blood
spilled in patterns suggesting hypothermia –

also, don't forget the caliginous cedars with raised roots
and boughs, how they can slow a search, or how the supple
branchlets of deciduous trees can slip into ear canals,

like the one that punched a circle in his tympanic
membrane, left him breathless and bewildered,
lying calmly in a drift as though in a deep featherbed.

But, all excuses aside, most of this short day was wasted
battling the mind of winter; everyone suspecting shamefully
within minutes it was the body they looked for, not the man –

knowing everything before the report would be perfunctory:
a brief shot at resuscitation, a swathing of black limbs, another
attempt at trudging home in the snow to join a wife in bed.

QUESTIONS FOR AN ELDERLY GENTLEMAN

What is this genealogy you have laid down on the sidewalk
like fossilized finch skeletons from some string of islands?

and how many squirrels do you think die of old age, falling from
the branches and hitting the ground with nut-choked cheeks?

and other than the scent of fruit, of livestock, of her hair held up
in loose braids with silk knots, can you remember home?

and in the navy, do you think they really only guessed direction
by the strips of sun and wind that lay across the deck?

and was it just in time for Halloween, the year you realized
the world was ugly: hunchbacks shuffling through the leaves?

and have you been here before, perhaps recently, and it has just
slipped your mind like a name on the tongue?

and when your wife withers, shaking in a chair, your hand on her
fluttering breastbone, how do you keep living a myth made for two?

and do you feel that getting lost here has been at all similar to
the moment of surprise and regret a bird must feel hitting a window?

and is there any point in noticing that some leaves cling longer
to the tree than others; that some apples fall in January?

and if your pictures of her could speak, what could they possibly
add to a thousand words?

and when you first saw the sea, did it look to you like a hem
for the wide skirt of sky or was it a darker day?

and tell me: will all conversation, even between the stupid and
the bored, deepen when there is really nothing left to say?

and what must it be like in a family plagued with cancer, when
tumours bloom more often than children and grow twice as fast?

and have you ever eaten a winter cherry when the pit is frozen,
the flesh so black it is easily disrobed with your tongue and palate?

and do you recognize this house? or this one? or this?

The Bats

As the lakeside cottage slips into the plum of dusk,
the fir trees and cedars darkening the rocks,

mosquitoes and bats rise with the moon,
silhouetted over the deck in brief bursts,

black wings against a sky like the deepest vein –
and in the deck chairs below, cottagers pull sweaters

up around reddened necks, roll pant legs down
over fishing-wet ankles –

city-folk, convincing themselves after a day casting
on the shore that they are simply unsure

of the chill in a northern summer evening, or suspicious
of the hidden whine of insects, or taking

sensible precautions against sparks from the fire –
but truly it is a doubt of what intentions beat above,

the clicks like those of a disapproving tongue,
the sweeps and dives into the airspace

about their heads, the occasional brush of leather
against an exposed scalp –

it is some instinct to duck and cover
they're learning to use, a natural tendency to make

their jugulars scarce, to pull heads down
between shoulders even though

everything they've learned tells them the predators above
are only feeding on what's feeding on them.

The Bird

I know what's hidden
under your thick coat of feathers –
the secret to your partnership
with the wind.

I called the bluff
on your impressive bulk
and stripped you
down to the essence
of your skill at flight –
but that skinny body,
the nervous, streamlined beak,
180-degree neck,
the slight, powerful muscles
about your shoulders and back
all hinted me wrong.

It's the legs
that betrayed you –
thin as thread and
knotted into tiny rosettes,
virtually weightless,
they are contracted to the ground,
only holding onto the earth
in the absence
of a pleasant sky.

You see, I have watched you
relaxing near the air –
seen you cross your legs
over each other

in a careless fashion,
spied you tying them
into a stitch before
stretching them straight,
before pushing away the planet
and having the wind,
visible through the sudden
presence of falling feathers,
blow you away.

The Third Ewe on the Left Behind the Nativity

When one of her sisters nosed up to the manger,
she did as well, hoping for a meal of grain, spring grass,
a lick of salt, or even, considering the season,

the placenta of a lamb being shared by
its mother: nothing more than something to eat,
where nothing other than food had been before –

but when she broke the woolly wall of those
next to whom she slept, she was disappointed,
exhaling her hot breath on an inedible human child.

Back in the fall, when the days first became colder,
sheep started disappearing, one every third morning –
the innkeeper or his wife arriving with a long knife

and sleep in their eyes, working black fingers
into hocks, under ribs, making a fist of wool behind
the fattest ewe's ears and dragging her off,

bleating in the steaming air, leaving the rest
to cower by the back wall of the stable. She, like all
her kind, had been a follower for as long as she

could remember: was used to moving like birds
in flight, the title of leader constantly shifting,
reserved for whoever happened to be in front –

there was less thinking involved that way, no need
to remember who was who, more attention left
for foraging and chewing, for waiting out the hours

until one of the humans came to either pour feed
in the trough or drag a sibling off under the blade.
And while, back when the flock was larger, the odds

of any visit seemed to favour her being fed,
with no mind for rhythm she grew to expect only
dinner, even as their numbers declined. Yet still,

perhaps by some intuition of fear, she, like the others,
willingly followed anyone but a man with a knife –
huddling instead in the straw of the stall,

waiting for the innkeeper to return with bloody hands
and a fork of grass: her tiny memory
already adjusting to the population change. And when,

with the weather warming and more men
than ever entering the mews, no food
was brought nor any sibling pulled away –

she was confused. And, as the men pushed
through the stable with the same breath,
laying unpalatable gifts by the man-child's side,

the flock, now dwindled to three, watched –
the third ewe from the left eyeing the procession,
sitting quietly apart from where her sisters

lay curled together for safety and warmth,
chewing on nothing, half-lidded as though
from boredom, yet secretly hopeful.

She was waiting patiently for the long night

of visitations to end and morning to come,
waiting to see if any of the assembled remembered

to bring offerings other than baubles for the child,
waiting for what she remembered
as important and inevitable –

for the flock to be fed or culled as always,
for some sedge or a handful of millet to be meted
out, for one of their number to be dragged off

like yesterday and the days before, bawling:
taking its small, but predictable, place in history.

Chasing Sky: A Great Lakes Photographer's Manual

She's taken to fleeing her home during
the worst weather, to chasing the sky
by playing dead in the bush –
      lying half-buried amid trilliums

and ferns, tucked quiet among pine
needles and the hollow skeletons of birds.
Keeping her teeth parallel to the earth,
      she lets her eyes pull in the clouds

  from between the branches –
              a harvest of silk webs or
the greyest wheat left through a winter.
   Everything comes to her this way,

    as easy as the ground passing
below or draughts pushing by above:
                  only she can be still.
Lightning, anvil crashes of thunder,

   or clear blue falling ever upwards –
         her eyes spin like lenses,
      like the angriest air picking up
leaves, bones, the homes of other families

    and smashing them into black soil.
   Even the blind can photograph the sky,
         she thinks,
      even the dead can walk on water –
   when all they're trying to capture
                  is infinity.

Mayflies in Autumn

My wife wakes frightened from a dream where mayflies
are crawling from the lavender scar on her abdomen,

the operation last winter having taken part of an ovary
along with twin cysts the size of mangoes –

she has been reading Freud again and is worse for it,
but won't listen to me when I tell her.

A bi-manual exam through the incision revealed dermoid cysts,
the surgery report read when we snuck a look

two weeks into the recovery, *a conjoined toxic fluid sac*
and endometriosis against the rear of the uterine wall.

(All this before thirty –
                    who can blame our family doctor
for diagnosing pregnancy during a routine physical.)

Left was an *ovarian remnant* on the right side and
a *migrating stitch* that allowed two hematomas

to let for days, blood welling the colour of black plums.
The events leading up to the dream are textbook,

at least as far as Freud is concerned, the bastard –
the diagnosis of gestation, the blood tests, ultrasounds,

the hushed guesses at every kind of growth imaginable,
three months on a waiting list, the operation, recovery,

the late-autumn weather, the dimpled line on her belly where
something that grew inside her has so obviously been removed.

A RUSTLE IN THE BUSH

A rustle in the bush stops us cold,
your raised hand a hole in the stars,
signing our conversation

to a stammer of crickets.
There is a sound of movement
from the woods behind the garden.

At night the flowers lose their colour
taking the shapes of hunched strangers
in the grey tangle of a deep bed,

heads dipped low toward the sheets,
leaf arms loose until morning.
In the taller grass near the edge of the pond,

a cat crouches, betrayed by its domesticity
and eyes, the reeds swaying around it
are quiet as witnesses.

I'm trying to tell you about my eye,
how when the light dims suddenly
one iris can't keep up with the other,

staying contracted, pinholed, expanding slower.
I'm saying I go blind on one side every time
you block the light by leaning in to kiss.

You laugh, tending the peonies,
their massive heads lolling drunkenly,
reintroducing yourself in the dark,

shaking petals hello, letting ants crawl
onto your hand and in between your fingers.
The honey dew you rubbed on your

nails attracts them, you say.
When I'm drunk, I explain,
everything seems occasional, the world

seasonally fragile, more momentary than
your peonies, more fleeting than your ants.
When I'm drunk my eyes focus

with the speed and accuracy of a cat.
It is a survival mechanism.
Rustles in the bush interrupt us again.

The cat raises its hackles, slits its eyes,
the ants drip from your fingers and
your hand moves up to cut holes in the night.

My eye slowly widens in the dark.
It's the movement of the ants,
you whisper, that separates the petals.

Is it the sound of something leaving
which stops me from replying,
or the heavy stumble of someone
coming home.

THE DEAD ARE DRINKING AT MY DOOR

The dead are drinking at my door, quiet and greatly respectful,
waiting without knocking, without fuss, without stumbling
through the walls. They linger outside the washroom
with the air of gentlemen drinkers, standing in the hall under
their own curling, yellowed photos, bridging the gaps
between us with phantom pub songs I've only recently learned,
with pint glasses, with a brew that pours and swallows smooth.

My mother's father, Tank-Sergeant James, is dressed in uniform,
buzzcut head, half-lidded eyes, maple leaf on his shoulder,
a thick cigarette dangles from the side of his mouth.
He holds a rifle under his arm, a bottle in each fist, looking at me
like he needs a light. A bullet hole in his leg is wrapped
in bandage – oozing. *I bled for thirty years*, he says, lifts a bottle
to his lips and fades, becoming the grey tones of a colourless photo.

My other grandfather, Victor, is dressed for the Orange parade,
his July Twelfth best – stained, creased flat, his face
a stumbling kilter of pride, of wailing song. My father never
knew the man, he died when dad was only a child. I look at him
standing there swaying and think of what a long line of drunks
I have to live up to. He reaches in his jacket for a flask, pours me
another. He smiles, revelling in the final hours of his march.

My dad, nineteen, on the deck of a ship, grease between his fingers,
dirt under his thick nails. Someone behind has called him and
he's half turned to go, but stopped as if looking back at me.
Son, he says, and I can hear his Belfast for the first time,
got to go, the police expect me to be in by eleven. I laugh
as he slowly begins to pixilate, freezing into the father I know
from pictures, becoming the myth that became the man.

They've each come to see me off, have a few pints,
get their pictures taken with the next in line and have a final
toast, one to me now that I am old enough to stand their chill.
They've each come to see me go, filter themselves one by one
through my liver and kidneys, slide from me, steaming
onto the ground. Smiling, I look at my glass, slowly swirl
the throwaway sip of beer, then move to close the door.

But Dad, I call before he is completely fixed and he stops
with his back to me. *You're not dead yet*. His shoulders slide
low – he looks over one at me. *Check your head, son,
I'm not his ghost*, he says, cocking a thumb
at his wrinkled photograph, *I'm yours*.

                                        I remove the chain
and with a breath of air from the hall, push open the wood.

The dead are drinking down my door. The three a.m. bangings,
the footsteps, the flushes, the broken mirror where I stood
looking at myself for an hour, pointing and laughing out loud.

The Interview

It has taken me ten years to get a suit this good,
but on the streets of New York with a garment bag
over my shoulder, I can't find anywhere to change.

At home you wear your new white robe like a pelt
stolen from some larger, much longer, animal –
perhaps a pale squirrel or stoat or muskrat.

The night bus to here is twelve hours of a colicky baby
screaming with the last of its throat – it is a humidor
in which tuberculosis is stored for future epidemics.

At thirty I am interviewing in the most targeted city
in the nuclear world for a job I am loathe to do –
my life is traceable by things I've failed at, and you.

Eight hours I sit in a bar that bears my name,
waiting out the afternoon until the company
has time enough to see my wrinkled jacket and tie.

Our friends complain that, suddenly, here we are –
and they're right in a way – but while life's been quite some
time in arriving, I suspect we've generally lived it all.

I suppose some moments are best left skipped, but
believe time only really speeds up when everything
you have to look forward to has already passed you by.

In a soiled toilet on the lower tip of Manhattan I change
between two mirrors, suddenly aware of the impression
of infinity, myself repeated over and away –

yet I am foiled in even this almost moment
by the limits of my poor vision and
the blockage of sight created by my own opaque head.

A knock on the door – an impatient young woman
whose apathy I've only just begun to experience –
words rest on my tongue with the foulest tequila

and I hold them there to see how long I can stand
before swallowing all three. I want to think of you as only
a stone's throw away, but I know that really depends

on both the size of the stone and the size of the man.

THE TRAIN

From the country I take the train,
a seat against the direction
of travel –
the roadside slipping by
slowly at first,
green at first,
then blurred and grey.

The birds flying towards me
are pulled away into the distance.

I slide into each city
as if leaving –
the familiar landscape
running away from me
and everything new creeping
up behind.

NOSTALGIA FOR THE SECOND JUST PAST

Do you remember how we wore our hair –
look at the way it fell, those silly locks
much thicker or thinner than now, more coloured,
more spiked, more coiffed, or less –
our beards trimmer, longer, heavier
or not covering much of the face, and they still
hadn't grown shaggy quite yet, or they had,
or they were perhaps not even there at all.

And those awful clothes, can you recall who
might have thought of pants like that,
of that colour for shirts, of how collars hung,
weren't present, of the priest-look,
the pauper-look, the academic with patches –
that we did not see how anachronistic,
how foppish, how military we appeared
is only a witness to the immaturity of our day.

Diversion, what there was of it, its abundance,
was that of a simpler time, more intense,
slapstick, tragedy, romance, ironic reference –
how did these things entertain us, enrage us,
so grainy and false, so true we shook our heads
and held our bellies, pounded fists in anger –
those brilliant, stilted, subtle actors working
with our empirical, absurd, jaded minds.

Those homes, what were we thinking –
form over function, function directing form,
the mess of vertical, horizontal space,
the architecture of boredom, cladding for the eye,

did we have no shame when we first thought
to decorate, did we have no taste –
everything so monumental, disposable,
a testament to the ages crumbling around us.

And politics, gentle beast, who could have predicted
the rise of fascism, democracy, lazy communism,
of the environmental vote or an anti-male movement –
we were savages, enlightened, the envy
of every civilized nation, a laughingstock
to the world, a beacon, an example, blind mindless
followers, automatons and anarchists, the breath
of all ideas made real by touch of cold.

O, but please tell us that the art said it all,
said nothing with purpose, without meaning,
is a record, an archive, the simplest of lists –
tell us it said what we were saying with
the permanence of paper, canvas, stone, so we
can at least be satisfied where we are, if not
where we've been, and for once in the history
of our species, live somewhat unashamed.

Here, where shadows of harvest clouds slide over
the field (the unturned corn stumps browned
and mowed into fingerless gloves) –
the abandoned house squats
with its black vandals' eyes,
stretching a gravel tongue
down to the concession –
and while their parents have told them
never to disturb an empty home unless
prepared to care for its children,
there is still a path snaking up
the overgrown hill (every teen in town
knowing what the dirty mattress
in the kitchen is for) –
because by September the drive-in is closed,
the school bells are clearing,
and dew in the park is almost cold
enough to be frost –
and though the walls are yet solid,
the stairs are rotted out and rats
have taken over the upper bedrooms
(scratching away through
even the most urgent lovemaking) –
and winter still pays visits,
knocking shutters, banging doors,
ushering in a sky mostly unsuited to blue –
and as the first rains shake chips of rust
from the ruddy pickup truck
on blocks in the yard, the roof takes up

leaking where it left off in the spring,
setting everyone to shivering –
even the rats knowing there is only two degrees'
difference between being here and not.

Pressure

I have a suspicion that volcanoes
sometimes explode from frustration
as well as pressure –

a need to express silence
with hearts inherited from the stars.
I often find myself the twisted

core of every mountain –
threatening, bleeding knots of stone,
shaking the planet like bedsheets,

then rocking to sleep in pools of rainwater.
It's waiting through life
with the indignity of a fault line

that's been the hardest.
That the words would elude me –
that they would dare.

III

I suddenly can't remember the text –
did Mary hold Jesus to her breast
to feed? was she bare to the waist in public?

and was Felicité the name of the maid
in Madame Bovary, the one who stole sugar
from the sideboard and ate it alone in her bed?

and what was the deal with Chiron, that bit about
the poison arrow striking his centaur hide
and sending him into a flight of constellation?

O Sagittarius! O Nostradamus! O Census!
Where are my predictions?
I was promised a few things in the seventies

and have yet to receive them –
I can only remember what I myself have written,
like a youngster with his first publication,

flipping past all the good pieces to his own.
Was it the Germans who were the bad guys?
the Koreans? the Iraqis? the Canadians?

Did Abraham actually kill his own son
or did he, Isaac, and Ishmael
go on to build the Kaaba at Mecca?

This I know: that little poor girl, Oliver Twist,

she just wanted a wee bit more food –
and the man who wrote her suffering and denial

now hangs upside down with the Devil,
turning as though he were a goose on a spit.

LIBRARY

Maybe you know how
to live in a way
that isn't just about breathing,
but I don't –
so please: reserve this
space for me.

        (Rest here a moment
        without thinking)

In what manner you choose
to keep your books:
I know this little part of you,
hold it sacred –
it's your other secrets,
if any, that are not safe with me.

Despite the Hunger and Delicious Taste

Despite the hunger and delicious taste of it,
knowledge frightens me –
I don't *want* to know how lightning works,
or gravity, or the speech-dance of bees.
Cuneiform markings on clay tablets should,
in my opinion, have stayed unreadable –
there would still be wonder, no disappointment
in the boredom between farmers.
I want to live without an awareness
that day and night are simultaneous,
without the ability to reach the white beaches
of Greece on a day's notice,
without the surety that thoughts are *not*
created and housed in my heart.
I want to believe that a cold spread of fear
that feels like déjà vu *is* déjà vu,
that when cats stare and hiss at nothing
they are actually confronting something,
that the red and purple spots left floating after
staring into a light are visions.
Is there no recourse for the simple soul
who won't let himself think in allegory –
the impregnation of women by the sun,
the healing properties of musical instruments,
that the sea was once stirred to procreate
by the consumption of severed testicles?
What I'd give to exist
in a state of perpetual ignorance
of things like the distance between stars,
perhaps *hundreds* of miles above –
or to live thinking the moon has a first name

and children, that they fall in the rain
to be raised by her lover, the sea –
that sometimes when she touches the hills
in the distance someone is crushed –
or that a companion sits there,
some ancient shepherd or dirty satyr
waiting to greet her, to help ease her
creaking bones down into a wide bed of earth.

Cassandra Complex: A Still-Life Suite

1: Young Woman Moving Between the Buildings

How can you walk with your head down,
is this what you learned in university –
to avoid stares, to navigate packs of private school
boys let out from detention, to pace blindly
while underlining aphorisms
                        in a philosophy book –

have you ever *seen* the people drawn to a class
on tragedy?

Was it too late when he asked you to run away
with him, and had you perhaps forgotten where
                    away was or how to run –
please remember that history for some people comes
with an eraser, and that, like all unwitting thugs,
he spoiled what he stood for by becoming
a parody of his own beliefs?

Between your steps are pauses filled
with everything before words –
would it be any comfort to be told that leaving
is a skill you can pick up again
                    at certain points on the road?

2: Young Man Looking Out from a Coffee Shop

Your hand is yellow almost to the wrist,
the fingers cracked at the prints from wind
funnelled down the streets –
your teeth are uneven and dark as ochre books

lined up on a crooked red shelf –
yet your face remains clear and new
as a bowl of milk
hours before or after a kitten has dined.

Memory has delayed you so little, yet still
you sit, a limp palm over the mouth
of your words as though testing whether
                it is Aphrodite
or an echo in the window that mocks you –

and I, also in the path of my own voice,
must restrain myself from calling out –
Look around, see what year it is!
Soon it will not be.

3: Man Idling at a Red Light

After all these years you still forget yourself.
Like Orpheus –
use your thumbs for music, not to smudge
the edges of everything, checking if it's fresh.

A thing of such intense beauty,
                          she made
both the elderly and the unborn curse
their random allotment of time –

but don't expect her to be waiting for you
            on the other side –
be satisfied that finding her in this life
was chance enough.

O my brother, think back! what memories
we share have drifted so far apart –
reality, it seems, is a relative thing,
particularly between us.

4: *Woman Walking in the Lee of a Pier*

You stand above the break with a face
that, like the hidden moon, has looked down
on your life with a certain disinterest.

You are not expected to see this –
the water moves too fast here for reflection
and your mind is tired of thinking.

Trust me when I say, it is common
to sometimes feel you couldn't even write
the alphabet if you wanted –

that it is too predictable, that you can't make
a story with a known ending exciting,
that, besides, it's been done before and better.

Let me tell you what I've discovered
the answer *isn't* –
to quit hoping someone better will come along

and finally just settle for yourself.

5: Middle-Aged Woman Reading Scripture on the Bus

Your body now points in only one direction
and your face, so full of the past, has grown hard –
mouth pulled down at the corners,
eyes creased like the spine of the book
you sit thumbing through, seemingly
unsurprised by what's within.
With the text held conspicuously high, you peek slyly

over the gilded edge as though dying
to be caught at something like this for a change,
as though checking whether anyone has noticed
you or your new-found holiness –
yet from time to time, even in your fakery, a parable
seems to catch you, drawing your attention inwards,
rolling your eyes up and back as though to say –

                              Now you tell me.

O if I could only explain how hard it has been to watch
you reflected in the window without sidling up,
without reassuring you the details of your life
aren't exposed on the thin lines framing your mouth,
without leaning in the manner of strangers who,
having shared a decent author, can whisper mischievously –
                    Hey, want to know how it ends?

6: Middle-Aged Man Leaving a Butcher's Shop with Nothing

Are you thinking back to a country where you couldn't
dig the dirt with your toe without uncovering
                              something of value –
where even a child's shovel and pail had the potential
to be mythically significant?

Isn't it that you want so terribly to be part of any story,
even a tragedy, that you are willing to have
your organs eaten by any bird, to roll the smallest
of stones anywhere, to be killed by any woman
regardless of whether she has borne you children?

If we spoke the same language, I might ask questions like –
                    why did you mistake acquiescence
for the fifth element? how will you survive history without
a middle for your life? when you finally decide to go to war
for her, do you think she'll still be young enough to care?

7: Elderly Woman on a Bench

Your quarter profile still looks
to youth like the second or third reflection
of a mirror, but the damp at the corners
of your face dates you –
the ribbons of many a bloodless death.

Shivering as I pass, I cough
in hopes of seeing you move.

O to be so immersed in memory
that even sound is lost,
drawn like water through dark soil,
back into your eyes.

8: Old Man Waiting at a Corner

Motionless you stand without breath
shoulder-deep in the swell
of hurried people, as though lost
or choosing between silent belief
and simple waiting –
is it only by the shadow stretching out
from the mast of your heels that you
can believe the sun is in the west?

Moments past! the sleeves of your shirt
are sewn shut, a wife's memory hangs
like a sword over you, the smoke
        that once curled

from your blunt yellow fingers
is suddenly exhaled like a stream of moths
over a bivouac's flame –
a dusty breath of wings leaving you
as though startled, as though waking,
as though you just sat up
from some dark water
struggling to remember how to breathe.

CLOCK, COMPASS, AND SWORD

Like Damocles, there are young courtiers
around today who could use a lesson in subtlety –

amateur sycophants looking to compete with the greats
in games of fawning, kowtowing, and toad-eating.

If only there were tyrants generous enough to match –
Dionysius having been lost long ago to his own peril.

There is a moment of death for every tick on the clock,
our fantasy despot would say at the early-evening feast,

hanging his sword by a single tress above the adulator,
and one for every point on the compass –

think of each space between the marked seconds
and bearings as the span of a life.

And as the blade rocked above the perspiring bootlick,
our dictator would slowly return to his seat saying –

Sometimes I grow tired and, it generally being past
my bedtime, I wonder if when the hands marking my lives

finish their rotation of the timepiece they will begin
anew, coursing through the hours and directions forever.

It's then I often ask myself, he'd note significantly,
slipping into his chair and sipping from an elegant glass,

if it does all just begin again, what's the point?
These days, a hush might descend on the banquet,

the assembled looking uncomfortably into their plates
as though remembering their own early years spent

scrambling for the eye of those in stations above them –
but for fun, let's pretend it isn't today, and that the feast

continues in raucous courses, only our young Damocles
silent for once, afraid to move or even open the mouth

so suited to talking himself into, and out of, favour –
the clock, compass, and sword all pointing in one direction.

Jonny and the Fish

The last thing I might have expected from Jonathan
was an ability to clean a fish, and so ruthlessly –

he's a delicate sort, for an Australian, works gathering funds
for the unemployed, wears clothes from shops

where people dance in the ads, has a nice watch, good teeth,
a sensitive man's goatee, the start of a balding trend –

but there he is, doing it, sawing the head off my fish
right in front of me (and I claim no macho superiority here,

after years away from the docks, I couldn't even take hooks out
the many wee ones caught before this, the flapping spines

of tiny rock bass jabbing holes in me like a leatherpunch) –
first he whacks it with a heavy wood spoon from the cottage,

then holds down the last of its twitches with one big paw
and digs in just behind the gills with a knife designed

for cutting fancy garnishes –
and the blood that comes over his hands, and the incision

he makes down the belly, and the way he rips the guts
out and discards them behind him in the weeds,

these are things I just never thought I'd see Jonathan doing –
the nice Jonathan who hates being called Jonny,

the Jonathan who listens to intellectual Australian pop music
and strong female vocalists, the Jonathan who laughed

with me, both of us totally clueless yet obviously obligated
to laugh, at a joke about Wittgenstein made in a pub –

but then, I suppose, he's been at the cottage five days longer
than I have, and has a head start on shaking everything else off.

It Always Rains on Remembrance Day

I realize these words will
hound me forever,
but there is something
you should know –
I can't yet dismiss
every nice sunset
as pollution,
or describe the newest
Hollywood starlet as a strange
experiment in eugenics,
or see the scandals of
America as simple ignorance –
you must understand
I am in love with the fact
that there is still
a place on the planet
with a name like
The Ivory Coast,
and the way angels
are making a comeback
in a time of aliens,
and how dolphins have
to choose to breathe,
and continue to do so –
when even the Vatican
stays open on Sundays,
or when gold pens
are being sold to the rich
in jewellery stores,
or when the cathedrals
of Europe have coin

operated lighting –
I tell you this because,
though I know
we can't blame ourselves
tomorrow for thoughts
we have today,
I am sometimes ashamed
it is only these things
that keep me from speaking
as an echo might –
and hoping maybe this
is the first Remembrance Day
I won't forget.

ESCAPING LAUGHTER

The first time I was unsure
of a woman's laugh
was when I was twelve –
trying out on the schoolyard
soccer pitch, mud and bruises
worn like a uniform,
the boys crashing into
each other like blind birds.
I had trotted to the sideline
where the coach paced
near the ranking board –
my name three from the top,
a small white chit
pinned to the plywood
like a broken tooth
barely left in a bully's victim.
I looked to where some girls
sat braiding and said to
my favourite Jennifer,
First Team, Inside Left –
that's good in soccer.
Behind her hand her teeth
were sparking,
above it her eyes held mine
then squinted out at the field.
Her laughter came short
and hard, like it was escaping
from somewhere under her chin.
I backed out into the safety
of the rough scrimmage
on the shaky legs of a survivor.

THE FORMER CONTENDER CONTEMPLATES HIS REFLECTION IN A MIRROR

Have I reached such an age already,
one where I am beginning to despise the body
I wear in favour of its memory,
a memory which may or may not be reliable –

I was a soccer halfback, right-winger in minor
league hockey, a judo champ, at least
at the hinterland level: somewhere
I have the medals to prove these things –

but the cross that used to split my abs,
the hard runnels of flesh that swept sweat
down my pecs and over my biceps,
the dimpled musculature of my back –

all these trophies are going, going, or gone,
leaving just photos of me in the local paper,
holding a ball, stick and gloves, standing
on a podium in brown belt and white ghi –

photographic evidence that seems less impressive
than I recall, corroborating only the various
small-time accomplishments and pursuits
I abandoned for epiphany and illumination.

I remember a sturdy, V-shaped body
something like on the men in advertisements,
but bigger: cut and polished and ready
as a loaded gun for anything thrown its way –

well, perhaps not so violent, but insidious: there
it is in my mind, that body, fooling me daily
into believing I can take the stairs two at a time,
that I can still swing my wife around in bed –

that I can join the kids down the street
in a game of pick-up without stretching,
that I am not too far off the chiselled, grimacing
men of the billboard underwear ads –

yet despite how I cling to them, these memories
are turning out to be untrustworthy, unfixed,
maybe growing in size like fish stories or
atrophying like underused muscles –

they are the little lies I tell to get through
to the end with some self-respect: I was good,
I was beautiful, I did important things,
if I'd kept at it, I could have been a contender.

Thunder in the Hollows

Sometimes thunder cuffs
the city below the horizon,
and rib-shaken, I am
trembled upcountry –
quaked back to the wooded farm
where we shared flowerbeds
and green fields –
where rain pounded the alfalfa
without grief, pocked the pond
for long moments, beat new craters
amid hoof-records in the riding
sand, smoothed out the footprints
we pressed into soil –
a land cleared of marks
so that no one could see how close
we once stood.

Yet when the sky lights itself,
I remember our trip
to the desert, away from
everything green –
how the glassy tubes of fulgurite
snaked like planetary blood clots,
knobby legs of lightning
wheedling through the evenly
spaced grains of earth.

Rain

the winemaker's rain falls like fat green grapes
the horse's rain advances in pellets of oats on the field
the student's rain is a hail of red erasers at lunchtime
the father's rain comes and goes
the stone's rain sounds of
the wind's rain introduced angles to the world
the banker's rain dents cars in a barrage of coins
the runner's rain gets pounded underfoot
the pilot's rain begins in a sky that never falls
the tree's rain bends under force from the wind
the moon's rain dots the I of creation
the photographer's rain is slanted lines of solid water
the writer's rain sounds of typewriter strikes
the teacher's rain hangs suspended like coloured chalk dust
the singer's rain runs up from the throat and passes the lips
the traveller's rain falls all over the planet
the astronaut's rain will arrive from the stars
the canine's rain is a hail of yellow fangs in the mouth
the mason's rain flies from under the hammer
the baby's rain rattles from the mobile clouds
the chickadee's rain is a sudden burst of feathers
the illusionist's rain has dis/covered/membered/appeared
the mother's rain holds long inside her
the priest's rain may or may not be there
the reporter's rain has caused much damage
the farmer's rain is family invited to dinner
the marshal's rain always gets its man
the river's rain is a sleet of new children hungry for movement
the wind's rain introduced angles to the world
the rose's rain beats petals into thorns
the miser's rain gets hoarded in bell jars

the artist's rain is slick blue on the canvas
the engineer's rain makes much sense for the planet
the pistol's rain travels straight through the heart
the sister's rain is hand-me-downs from the brother
the brother's rain glosses the eyes of the sister
the feline's rain is indifferent to those it falls on
the lord's rain is the oldest of weapons
the fat man's rain hangs guiltily at the back of the tongue
the enemy's rain chambers itself in the gun
the mayor's rain is short-lived and perfunctory
the television's rain falls in a hundred different channels
the radio's rain requires too much effort
the star's rain raises Braille from the night
the worm's rain pulls itself from the ground
the puddle's rain is the beginning of all clouds
the cloud's rain tears from the end of a thousand faces
the weeper's rain is cousin to the darkest sky
the wind's rain introduced angles to the world
the planet's rain falls less in expectancy of more destruction
the hermit's rain holds itself for the day he steps from the cave
the dancer's rain curls drop around drop as it leaps to the earth
the sun's rain is half a rainbow circling the eye
the prophet's rain is the beginning
the philosopher's rain is the middle
the scientist's rain is the end

An Egyptian Soldier on the Red Sea Swims Away from Moses

Even before the swells began to crash back in
I had a bad feeling about the situation, but under orders,
persisted as any good soldier would: pressed on

regardless of the high walls of black water groaning
and straining as though against the side of an invisible
but poorly constructed dike. So far ahead

we could never have caught them anyway, the excited
roar of the Jews, scrambling out of the trench
of sea, tipped off some engineers' instinct

in my mind and I began to divest myself of metal –
first my sword, then my shield, then bronze pauldrons
and the ringing helm of solid copper on my head,

even the gold trappings about my ears and waist
falling surreptitiously from the back of the chariot
and down to the ocean floor where they may,

for all I know, still rest to this day among the skeletons
and fish: rotting to a coral green in the salt of that angry
and insulted tide. While the callings

my people have embraced range from fishwife
to concubine, potter to soldier, farmer to Pharaoh –
every soul raised in the Delta, Egyptian or Jew,

knows the particulars of flooding: it starts with
starry signs that pock the pupil of sky, a foetid thickness
of air, a deep humming of insects,

the numeric significance of water growing as it trickles
through the dampening night. And, yes, while
at every phase of my denuding I mourned the loss

of my family's fortune, honour, and luck –
as the bound sea collapsed, its halves of water
rushing together like a majestic clap of hands or

siblings long apart, I was given a vision and embraced
my new position under the sun: that of prognosticator,
diviner, augur of water to cleanse the land –

the only Egyptian naked enough before the fist
of the Jewish god, the only one unidentifiable
in the roiling waves, the only one enough disguised

as human to be left floating, alive, head bare
under the burning Eye of Re –
tattooed arms free to strike out in any direction for land.

IV

The Unrecorded Life of Seamus Mé Féin

i: The Pits of Fruit Instead of Stones

Seamus, since you've been there already
your questions can be answered,
but know there is no guarantee things will happen
this way again, in this order, or at all –

and yes, before your first year ends your Catholic father
will leave you, his long face receding from the rails
of your pram, the grey streets and black
pinnacles of churches behind like curious people –

and then at age two you will skin your knee
on a brick that was once thrown through a window
in county Antrim, its owner having picked it out
of the rubble and made it a souvenir –

and when you enter the first form at five, your mother
will buy you new shoes made from hard leather
that will bite and scar your heels, but you'll love them
even as they eat the backs of your black stockings –

and at the start of your seventh year, you will befriend
a boy named Raymond, one of the black Irish,
his hair dark as cave, and the two of you will get lost,
then found, in a wood where the brake is over your head –

and at age nine you'll catch rumour of your father
who you will have passed unwittingly several times
on the street that very week: neither of you
noticing each other's eyes, nose, chin, or hair –

and then at twelve you'll kiss a girl named Margaret
for giving you the ruts of her apple, and it will last too long,
and the taste of her lips: sweet, wet flesh below russet skin,
will stay with you through every dream you ever have –

and at fourteen your mother's brother will force you
to the street where the Orangemen are having their parade
and make you march, the best of your childhood friends
hurling at you the pits of fruit instead of stones.

ii: The Abandoned Orchard

Seamus, there are things about your life
you haven't yet discovered –
for instance, unlike the average man

who stumbles about in his own immortality,
you have the ability to perceive
every brush with death you've ever had –

and once when you were just learning to walk,
you healed a three-legged toad
by touching it with a stick from an oak tree,

your mother never mentioning the event
to anyone but those in her prayers –
you can also make yourself bleed from any point

on your skin by sheer force of will,
something you will realize one Christmas soon –
and that time in the abandoned orchard

when you were frightened by the hoary trees,
their unpruned crowns yielding
a spotted harvest of wild sour apples, that time

when you climbed into the tangled branches
to eat the least-wormed fruit at the top,
that time you lost your grip and dropped

to the rocky soil below, breaking your hand
to break your fall: despite the metal in your life,
that was the moment you became a carpenter –

and Seamus, this indecision of yours has always
been fuelled by a buried memory
from your youth, one of lying by the hearth

in your mother's home,
and watching the heat move across your body.

iii: Tip on the Name of the Tongue

Seamus, because you deserve it on some level,
here is where your siblings all went:

Mary, one year younger than you, and Brighid, one older,
both ended up in Madrid teaching dance to the locals;

their shoes are worn through, three pairs a year,
a good life and they are still happy and together –

your brother Patrick died two years ago in Liverpool
of a barstool across the throat; his hands were callused

and cracked between the fingers, which tells
of good work, the kind he was fond of

and good at too; but the knuckles, all busted and swollen
to many times their natural size, may or may not

have been attributable to the wrench –
and Donagh, he lives in Brooklyn now, runs a small firm

dedicated to the production and sale of sheet metal;
his wife's name is Melanie, his children are Laura, Anne,

and Arlene, for your mother, whom they never met –
as for Evelyn, she lives in the south, in Galway,

has a small cottage on the cliffs, rents a room with marble
and dark furniture to an Indian man who flies in twice

yearly from Delhi, his heart near bursting with the stress
of selling motor cars, his head swollen with the book

he never writes while sitting facing out to sea –
and Sean, your favourite: he thinks of you often,

thinks of the others too, as you'd like,
even some of the younger ones he barely met;

he has a large dog of uncertain parentage, calls it Berlin
after a crush he had on a blonde woman

who moved to, and still lives, there –
Caitlín is convalescing in an asylum near Florence:

that traveller's flu she picked up back in Turkey
bred complicated pneumonia; she's been trying to find you

for some time as she's known since February last
she's been dying and wants to get on with it –

and Erin, the last to come and first to leave,
well he'll be dead twenty years on Saturday;

they say it was the cold of Canada that got him,
frozen like that in his tracks as he changed a flat

only minutes outside somewhere called Sudbury:
an awfully English-sounding place to go –

Seamus, they all have a name for you, and though
it's always spelled the same, they each pronounce

it differently: the weight of those wild countries,
the years and the fading memory of your younger face,

pressing down hard on the tongue.

iv: The Slowest Lighthouse Beacon

Seamus, but why torture yourself, you cannot change
a thing: everything will happen, or not,
with or without you, everything and nothing, all at once,
and your knowing will not help you a bit –

so, again, at sixteen a man your mother knows, but whom
you've never met, will arrive at the door with an address
written in black ink on a torn piece of paper and
your apprenticeship as a welder will begin the next day –

and when only seventeen you'll come home from a dance
so drunk you'll have shit your pants, and your friends
will leave you stinking on your bed, and in the morning
your mother will find you and laugh uncomfortably –

and turning twenty-one you'll flee Ireland, the fighting
between your childhood friends having frightened you,
and you'll follow first one brother's path, then another's
until, finding neither, a sister will hunt you down in Sydney –

and having returned at twenty-five you'll see *her* standing
on a rock near Cork, a tourist you'll make a citizen,
her belly soft from the space and scars of another man,
a child neither of you will ever ask after, or even mention –

and as you turn twenty-six, she will miscarry, then again on
your next birthday, and, in an attempt to help, you'll spend
years in the drink, and when you emerge bleary-eyed
at thirty, a son will have been born and be expecting a sister –

and at thirty-two, you'll meet a man on the street who says,
at first, his name is Malloy, then Sam, and that he's a pilot,

then a poet, a firefighter, a pirate, or an archaeologist, depending
on the drink, and the two of you will become great friends –

and at thirty-three you will wake one day in a barmaid's bed,
the pub below just waking; the ample fat of her arms and breasts
still and white, the sun creeping across the sheets
like the slowest lighthouse beacon warning away the fog.

v: Mortar, Stone, and Bucket

Seamus, if you'd married that woman from work, her nails
black as the factory floor, her face lined like yours,
wrinkles darkened with the soot, her womb a presence
between you as though already filled with child,

you'd have married anger: raucous laughter, a heavy
weight of father, a terrible fear of loneliness –
and if you'd married that girl from the corner, the clear-faced
one your mother forced you to church with years ago,

the one whose dress you once looked up as she climbed
the Morgans' tree ahead of you, you'd have married
sorrow: a family plagued by hidden poverty, lawsuits
and collectors, a sister who carries the gene for Down's,

the ghost of a perfect preacher who broke the cast
all men should be poured in –
and if you'd married your pretty teacher from middle school,
her skirts introducing the concept of curves

and buttons to your continentally drifting mind, her voice
like the brightest tone of a bell or the stillest
bowl of fresh milk, you'd have married the drink: a brother
who rests his beer on the toilet while thinking,

a sister who disappears for days at a time only to turn up
dishevelled and insulted at family gatherings –
and the booze would have been a well that never runs dry
for you *both*, its first taste a shackle with a chain never

longer than an arm's reach from the mortar, stone, and bucket.

vi: Head Hung and No Food in the Basket

Seamus, some things are harder to say than others,
and there are things you don't know you don't want to know;
but your voice, run so ragged and thin with pleading,
has made words of command –

be prepared: at age thirty-eight you will come home from
the foundry to discover your boy crippled in bed, having taken
a rock to the head, the doctor declaring him simple,
and he'll stay that way for the fifteen years it takes him to die –

and when thirty-nine you will be told by a fellow at the pub
that your wife was seen a few towns over with a bloke
he knows from Tara, and because the bar will go so quiet
you'll break his front teeth and deaden one of his eyes –

and then at forty you will see a look on the foreman's face,
know that he is a family man who's as hurt by all this
as you, that there was a time in his life when he went home
with his head hung and no food in the basket –

and at forty-one you will find hidden letters to your wife from
her sister, and even without a full grasp of the words you'll glean
what's coming and throw them in the fire, then thank God
the next morning a draft from the flue had breathed them back –

and two months after your forty-third year begins, your
daughter will look at you through tears and hate you for being
a man, and though you'll reach to touch her, your callused
hand will make her jump and you will never try again.

vii: A Shoe Full of Grain

Seamus, for years you have been walking
as though with a shoe full of grain –
circling away from home like the wavering
pulse of a bloody accident victim

who is still undecided about whether to return
to everything life had to offer;
growing in your intent, then shrinking –
for one so quick, it's odd that it has taken you

since birth to learn such a silly little thing:
that after years of mulling about looking for what
you really wanted, life may have turned out
to be a glass of water drawn from a well at home.

viii: No One With a Cup

O Seamus, where to begin, where to end when your asking
strays across the story like a blind man in the open;
your only promise now is that the light is growing,
and will be there when you look back –

so then, coming to the end, there will be age forty-seven
and everything it brings: your first year alone again,
a job at the mill cutting planks, the bottom of a bottle
used as a monocle, everything taking on funhouse shapes –

and forty-nine, the age your father never reached, nothing
will happen, nothing at all: nothing you will remember
but thinking and drinking, the smell of sleeping friends
and the deep warmth of a whore named Anne on winter nights –

and at fifty-five you will come to at a wake, your blazer
stained with the drink you have spilled on yourself; there will
be people you know, and some you don't, and they will all be
staring as though you've just said something profound –

and when fifty-nine, while meeting with your daughter who
is writing about her life for a magazine and wants to hear
stories of her mother, your parents and brothers and sisters,
you will start with a jump if even part of one comes to you –

and up on to sixty, you will feel something growing
in your head, will perhaps think it an idea: a craving,
a resolution to quit something for once, to find out where things
left off, to look up a few dead relatives; to look *her* up –

and in your final years, Seamus, words will come to you,
much as they had as a child, and they will fall from you

like blood from a wound; and because you have just awakened,
and because you are the last, there will be no one with a cup

to catch even the smallest sound as it hits the soil.

ix: Opened Like a Thief

Seamus, why is it important to know these things
when, if you'd only wait out the confusion,
the answers would stumble into you as though

you were leading them through the dark,
each clumsy question heavy with shadow –
think back: how foreign was *her* name when first

you heard it there in the heath, so American,
the consonants percussive as snares –
and remember *his* name, long and Irish, a name

without written equivalent, you once called him
father but forgot everything else, like his face –
and then there was the early memory of *her* face, wide,

dusted with sun, dappled even in the dark like the flank
of a horse, the ocean of her eyes holding you to her breast –
and remember *his* eyes, you both still children,

blackened like that from your fist or from playing
in the coal, a wedge of blue below his nails –
and what about *her* fingers, soft on your forehead

through your fever, mother standing over you both,
using your illness to teach her healing –
and then *her* belly waiting under the doctor's knife,

opened like a thief of whom the police remain unsure,
inside your curled and smuggled child –
and *him*, Seamus, *you*; before you go on,

do everyone a favour and please clarify: who do you
mean by *him*, and who do you mean by *her*?

x: Mouths of the Deepest Wells

Seamus, in answer to your last question,
I'm sorry, you'll be dying of cancer,
sunspots from your mottled skin having spread

to your liver and bones, then slowly up
into the deepest parts of your mind,
the black tumours opening like mouths

of the deepest wells –
and while they say every man calls
for his mother at death,

you will find that is a lie –
the name you call will be another's: *hers*,
the woman who you thought you found

years before when walking in the heath –
but as you age, you'll realize you never found her,
nor her you, even though it seemed

at the time she was waiting for you
on the path like a cutpurse in the night,
the blackjack concealed in her fist

invisible against the dark sky even
in its blurry downward arc towards your head –
yes, you'll be dying of cancer,

and you'll be alone, though not lonely,
everyone else simply having gone on already,
leaving their best wishes behind –

the knotted wood of your sister's cottage
around you, photos on the wall a canopy of black
and white leaves, your brothers and sisters,

parents and children, and your wife –
and though you'll think your mother's name,
at that very long final moment,

hers will come out, the sound
of your own voice surprising you,
setting you back into memory as though

it were a carriage made of your brittle bones
carrying you off to sleep –
you'll be dying, Seamus, and being born,

and when you speak her name,
you will hear yourself crying out
every name you've ever known,

all at once.

ACKNOWLEDGEMENTS

Some of these poems appear in the following journals: *The Backwater Review, Descant, Exile, Event, Grain, The Iowa Review, Ontario Review, Prairie Fire, PRISM international*.

Support towards the writing and editing of this book was provided by the Toronto Arts Council and the Ontario Arts Council.

The author wishes to personally thank the following people who directly affected the shape and production of these poems: Jonathan Bennett, Diana Fitzgerald Bryden, Peter Buck, Barry Callaghan, Anita Chong, Patrick Crean, Peter Darbyshire, Peter and Gena Gorrell, Michael Holmes, Adam Levin, Gabriel Levin, Wendy Morgan, Jack Muir, Richard Outram, Ellen Seligman, Don Summerhayes, Susan Swan, John Unrau, Paul Vermeersch.

Extra special thanks to the editors: Ailsa Craig (always the first reader) and Molly Peacock (for the press).